Super Savers

Train Your Kids to Become Financial Superheroes

Jeff Barnette

Super Savers:

Train Your Kids to Be Financial Superheroes

© 2020 Daily Dollar Finances.

All Rights Reserved.

ISBN: 9798623862594

Kindle eBook: B0864YS93J

For more information please visit

www.SuperSaversBook.com.

Disclaimer:

The information provided in this book is based on personal experience and is for informational purposes only and should not be construed as professional financial, accounting, or legal advice. Should you need such advice, please consult a licensed financial or tax advisor. The authors are not liable for any losses or damages related to actions or failure to act related to the content of this book.

For William and Anna

Table of Contents

Introduction 1

Chapter 1: Parental Responsibility 5

    The Necessity of Teaching Our Children 6

    The Mistakes We Make & How to Avoid Them ... 9

    Begin with the Basics 11

Chapter 2: Start Teaching Them Early 25

    Learning the Basics 26

    From Toddler to Teen 33

    Teach Your Children to be Super Savers 39

Chapter 3: Responsible Spending 45

    Intentional Spending 46

    Delayed Gratification 55

    Paying Cash Not Credit 63

Chapter 4: Paying it Forward 69

    Why Giving is Important 69

    The Act of Giving 76

Chapter 5: Supercharge Their Savings................... 79

    Compounding Interest 80

    Gifting for a Head Start......................................88

    Matching Contributions 93

Chapter 6: Going Beyond the Piggy Bank............. 97

    Giving Money a Job.. 102

Chapter 7: Money Lessons by Age........................ 113

    Teaching to the Learning Curve........................ 114

    Ages 3-5 117

    Ages 6-10 121

    Ages 11-13... 123

    Ages 14-18 125

    Ages 18+.. 126

Conclusion..131

Introduction

Train up a child in the way he should go: and when he is old, he will not depart from it.

Proverbs 22:6 KJV

As parents, we have a unique responsibility to pass down financial wisdom to our children. Kids don't inherently know what money is or how to handle it when they are young. They certainly won't care about saving any of it. What they do learn is by watching how their parents and other family members handle their own money. It is the parents' responsibility to set a good example of how to

Super Savers

responsibly manage money, as well as how to save and invest it for the future.

But what are parents teaching their kids these days about financial responsibility? It is unfortunate that many children today do not receive any real financial guidance, either formal or informal. This has become a topic of increasing importance as studies have shown the increase of debt taken on by the youth of today. Sound financial choices are something that you have to be ready to make, and most of our children are not prepared.

The average college student loan debt has increased 107% in the past decade, from 2009 to 2019, while their median credit card debt rose 31% since 2016 (*Federal Reserve and Sallie Mae, 2019*).

When it comes to college graduates, 11.1% of college graduates in 2019 have student loans in default (*US Dept of Education, Federal Student Aid, 2019*).

Introduction

The youth of today are rarely given any chance for formal instruction when it comes to financial matters. Most of their knowledge about money comes to them from more informal socialization sources, usually through observation of their peers, caregivers, and other influential adults in their lives.

A survey done by T. Rowe Price called *Money Confident Kids* reports that only 15% of the kids say that they frequently talk to their parents about money, while the survey also showed that over 19% rarely discussed or never learned even the most basic skills of creating simple budgets, comparison shopping, or understanding invoices (*T. Rowe Price, Money Confident Kids, 2019*).

One reason is that these skills are no longer being taught in schools. Another reason is that parents have to work longer hours, and sometimes both parents work to meet the household finances. The

Super Savers

kids aren't given the attention that they once were, and they need direction for their futures!

It still falls on us, as parents, to give them that direction. If we want our kids to succeed, we must train them for success. And as we grow further down this path of digital age finances, who knows... they may be able to sweep in and help us navigate the digital, while we train them to navigate the digits, like the superheroes they are destined to become... with our guidance of course.

Chapter 1: Parental Responsibility

"Money doesn't grow on trees!"

How many times have we heard this statement, or perhaps even used it ourselves? Unless they are taught otherwise, many children don't truly understand what is meant by this. It is the parent's responsibility to teach their children what this means—not only to simply understand it, but to prepare themselves for success later in life through the examination of it.

Super Savers

The Necessity of Teaching Our Children

Every parent understands the importance of money and teaching our children about it. At the very least, we teach them how to count pennies, nickels, dimes, quarters, and dollar bills. We teach them the value of each, how to combine them to reach certain totals, and how to accurately count the change we give or receive. At least the majority of parents do. Some don't even do that much, depending on the schools to teach our children these things. We are failing them.

Sometimes people don't think in terms of their children needing knowledge of how money works because they think they are too young to learn. But nothing could be further from the truth! If you think that your child is too young to understand the working concepts of money, I want you to consider the story of Warren Buffett, one of the most successful investors of all time and the CEO of

Berkshire Hathaway, a massive investment holding company.

Buffett's father thought that waiting until children were teenagers was too late to begin their training in how money works and was a great mistake in parenting. He taught his own son at a very young age and was a believer that children should be taught as early as preschool. By the time Buffett was six, he was already a businessman with a handful of working "small businesses."

He not only sold packs of Juicy Fruit chewing gum, magazines, and calendars door-to-door, but he also would buy a six-pack of Coca-Cola bottles for $.25 from his grandfather's grocery store, and then resell each bottle separately for $.05 each. This earned him a 20% profit on each six-pack.

Because of the way his father taught him, Buffett carried the tradition even further with his own kids.

Super Savers

The *"Secret Millionaire's Club"* was an animated children's series that he launched, featuring himself mentoring a group of students. There were 26 episodes in total, each teaching their own financial lesson. Some were more abstract, like how to make good decisions, or how to tell the difference between value and price, while others were more defined such as how credit cards work or tracking how and where you spend your money.

Buffett's father wasn't far off the mark. It has been scientifically shown that 80% of our brain growth as humans occurs by the time we are three years of age. Parents are usually the ones we turn to at such a tender age and where our first learning experiences come from. It is only right that we shoulder the responsibility of teaching our kids how to save and spend wisely. This isn't something that should be left to the schools to teach; we need to be far more vested in our children's futures. Take the time to train them in earning more and spending less... Train them to be Super Savers!

The Mistakes We Make & How to Avoid Them

We have already covered the first mistake that we often make as parents... assuming that our children are too young to learn about such a complicated concept. Our children have amazingly inquisitive minds, and the only way we encourage their brilliance to shine is to hone their inquisitiveness.

Start slowly, watch for their responses, keep your frustration to a minimum. If you can see that they don't understand the meaning of apples, switch to oranges. If oranges draw confused looks, try bananas. In essence, each of us learns differently. If we aren't getting through with one concept, try approaching that concept from a different direction, or switch to a related concept that might be easier to understand, and then later bring it back to the

Super Savers

concept you were trying to teach in the first place. It is just as frustrating for them as it is for you. More often than not, your children want your approval and for you to be proud of them. They will work to prove themselves, if you give them the chance... and your patience.

The second mistake is another that we touched upon, but sometimes it helps to speak plainly. There is no one more invested in your kids' future than you, their parents. We sometimes make the mistake in thinking that our children are learning money lessons in school.

However, in these days where schools are teaching to the Standardized Testing system in order to maintain their school's rating, and thus their influx of federal funds, there is very little being taught to our children in the financial areas. Even when they were teaching about money use, they still weren't teaching about important things such as value vs.

price, or credit cards and interest, or savings programs and how to implement and use them. These things need to come from us, as the parents, if we truly want our children to thrive.

Begin with the Basics

We all have wants and needs. It is up to us, as parents, to teach our children the difference between wants and needs, especially when it comes to money. We *want* that new video game. We *need* to have a home and food. It's important not to discourage wants, because those wants become a tool to drive us toward success. It is also important to place an emphasis on need over want.

By setting them up with even the most basic of understandings, we are putting our children on a path to success. If we never teach them these things and allow them to just lose themselves to video games, television, and constant play time, we lose

Super Savers

valuable time in training them how to gear up to be successful in life. The only thing they get from us then is a sense of entitlement, that everything will always be handed to them, and we all know the path of failure that develops from there. If we care about our children and want to do our best by them, we can't allow this to happen.

Start with the "Why?"

Teaching your children doesn't have to be complicated. The first step can be as simple as giving them an understanding of "Why?". Before kids can understand the concepts of money and how it works, it helps that they understand why they need it. Teaching them that pretty much everything in life costs money, from their clothes to their home, from their food, video games... to the utilities such as water and electricity, is giving the very earliest of the foundation needed for understanding, prepping them for success from the start.

Work as a Tool for Success

From there, it helps to give them an understanding of work and business, at least as far as being the tools to bring in money to pay for all the things they now understand costs money. This is why parents go to work and spend the long hours that they do away from home. We go to work, and for every hour that we work, we are paid money.

The same goes with businesses. While you aren't paid every hour for the work that you do, every sale that you make in business gives you a profit that is now yours to spend, or to put back into the business to make more money. The Warren Buffett example of buying six-packs and then selling them as individual bottles helps to serve as a good example for how you buy at a lower price and sell at a higher one to create a profit margin.

When we set our children up with an understanding of work, what it can do for us in life, and how far it

Super Savers

can take us toward our goals, we are setting them up for success. We are giving them the essential developmental skills that they will carry throughout their lives. This really has an impact when they are raised with these work ethics, along with a sense of money understanding and responsibility from an early age.

We are not just teaching them skills. These teachings give them more than just knowledge. They provide our children with structure and discipline that they can apply to their lives. We are training them for a lifestyle of success.

Once we have given them a basic understanding of work, we can move into encouraging them to earn those things they want in life. They can do chores around the house to earn money. They can offer to mow the neighbor's lawn, rake leaves, sweep or shovel their walkways, help a relative or family friend clean their garage to earn money for those things they want in life. It also sets the stage for learning to have more control over their lives and their future.

If you do want to give your children an allowance, make sure that it is tied to things that they must do to earn that allowance. If they are simply given the money, they become expectant that life will always just give them what they want, instead of having to earn it. You can make the allowance a set amount per week but assign a monetary value to each of the things you want them to accomplish for the week.

It doesn't have to be chores... it can be for studying "x" number of hours. They can earn a bonus for passing that school exam with a grade of "B" or higher. Set it up and assign whatever value you will, but the point is to stick with the structure, so that they understand the value of what it is they are doing.

Super Savers

Teach Them to Save

It doesn't matter the age, teaching your kids to save is a valuable lesson toward money responsibility. The younger they are, and the more visual you can make the savings, the better grasp they have as the money starts to grow in their piggy bank, or even a glass jar.

For older kids, starting a bank account is an option. It's not about what kind of account they open, although you can examine the options as part of their learning experience, it's more about the act of actually opening the account and depositing savings into it. It also doesn't have to be tied to any particular savings goal, although it can be.

For instance, you can set up their savings with the intent of their saving toward a particular item that they want... a video game, or a car. Or you could simply just set it up as savings to have on hand for the future—for instance when they turn 18. Another

Parental Responsibility

option to consider is to give them a goal of a certain dollar amount... $500, for example, and you can offer to either match every $500 they make, or to give them a 10% bonus... $50 for every $500 they deposit. Whatever you think best suits your own budget, and what would work to best help your child be excited by the lesson, choose a way to help them understand the value of saving for their future.

Since visual aides are often a great way toward better understanding, or even a reminder of what the goal is, there are several things you can try in order to help encourage and give incentive for what your children are working to accomplish. First, going back to the idea of a piggy bank or glass jar... Most piggy banks do not show the amount of money piling up inside. Thus, the idea of using the glass jar. It allows the child to visually see the money building up as they continue to contribute to their savings.

Super Savers

Another thought is to set up a marble jar. Figure out with your child how much the item is that they want, or what their monetary goal is that they want to reach through their savings efforts. This works even if they have the money going into a bank account. Based on the amount they are striving for, set a value for each marble. If they are trying to save $50, you might assign a value of $1 per marble. If they are trying to save $1,000, you might want to assign a higher value, such as $10, $25, or $50 per marble.

Put the number of marbles into the jar to show what it will look like when they reach their goal, and then draw a line with a permanent marker on the outside of the jar. Empty the jar and hang onto the marbles. Every time your child makes a deposit into their savings that is equal to the value set on the marbles, give them a marble to put into the jar. They now know that when their pile of marbles hits that line, they have reached their goal, and can watch for

Parental Responsibility

themselves how quickly they are moving toward their intended mark.

Another idea, which can especially work if your child has a specific item they wish to save towards, is to get a picture of the actual thing they are trying to save for. If you are using a piggy bank or glass jar, you can tape the picture to the jar, to remind them what it is that they are saving for, and to motivate them toward continuing to add to their savings to reach their goal. If the money is in a bank account, try taping the picture to the inside of their bedroom door, or another conspicuous place, so that they can see it daily, and be energized as they go throughout their day to add to their pile of savings and more quickly reach their goal.

Each child is going to be motivated in different ways, depending upon their learning style. Use what will best suit them, and of one thing doesn't seem to work, try another. The goal is to train them in the

Super Savers

dedication, responsibility, perseverance, and overall mindset that it takes to become a financial superhero for the success of their future.

The Lessons of Spending

Another valuable lesson in understanding money responsibility is to teach your children the importance of *how* to spend money. The best way to accomplish this is to take them shopping and help them actually *spend* their money. The first way we can help our children in learning how to spend money is to first help them become good decision makers.

Start allowing them to make their own decisions as to their preferences at a young age whenever possible. Do you want to wear jeans or shorts today? Discuss the weather with them and help them make their decision based on circumstances. Do you want to go to the park or lake today? The lake may require drive time that takes away from fun time, whereas the park is only a few minutes' walk away, allowing the child to have more fun time.

There doesn't have to be a reason for the choice either, it can be a decision based simply on preference… do you want to wear your green shirt or red shirt today? The goal is to help your child understand what decision-making is, and to be ready to make decisions whenever and wherever they may pop up in life. Learning good decision-making skills early on will transfer into making good decisions later when it comes to finances.

Emphasize the training on needs versus wants. It doesn't have to be about staples over entertainment. It can be something that comes up more in our daily exposure to advertising. Yes, you do need a pair of sneakers for school gym class, but you do not need Adidas… that is a want versus a need, and the value needs to be examined over other items that are wanted or needed in their lives.

Super Savers

It can also be an examination of features at that point too, which adds value to the decision-making process. Yes, you need running shoes for your after school cross-country running activity. Are the cheaper sneakers really going to be enough to get you by, or do you need those Adidas because they were developed for runners and the extra cushioning of the impact points where your foot hits the ground will actually prevent the shin splints you might get from regular, or less expensive running shoes? The lesson is that cheaper is not always better. It's going to cost you more in the long run if you don't get what is needed with the first purchase.

We'll be examining some of these concepts a little more later throughout this book. The main point through all of this is that there are simple ways that you can help your child grow into becoming a Super Saver, and to begin preparing for their financial future at a very young age. It is our jobs, as parents to show them the way, and then watch them grow into the role.

Chapter 2: Start Teaching Them Early

As we have demonstrated through our previous examples, starting your children on the right financial path is something that can be done at any age. Some of the shown methods can be started as early as age 3. As your child grows in knowledge, and in years, more can be added. This is not a single lesson, it is a series of lessons that we must stay on top of, in order to give our children a lifetime of value.

Super Savers

Learning the Basics

Some of the basics we have already examined are the "Why?" of money, the "How" we earn it, and the "What" we can use it for. We have covered some very simple ways for teaching earning, saving, and spending. So, let's take a look at some more ways we can teach our children throughout the years we are blessed to have them look to us for answers.

Set an Example!

First and foremost—be a good example! You can start by examining what your attitudes are about money, and how you use it yourself. Children learn most things by watching their parents and imitating what they do. If you want your children to develop good money habits, you must show restraint and wisdom in how you handle your own finances. If your children see you do comparison shopping, or putting something aside for a later purchase, they are more likely to naturally learn these things without you even having to say a word.

The University of Cambridge, UK did a study that showed that by the time they are 7, children have already formed their basic money habits. This doesn't mean that we can't change or break bad habits but be aware that those little eyes are watching you from early on. They watch when their parents argue about money, or when a piece of plastic is used for every purchase. It is up to us to set the example that we want our children to learn by and follow throughout their years.

Be Positive

With anything we teach our children, they respond best to the learning process and retaining information when we make it a positive experience. Make sure to offer lots of praise when even their smallest accomplishments merit it. When they have a setback, point out the good that they did before,

Super Savers

and how working harder can get them back on track. Teach them not to dwell on the negative, but to examine it for the ways that they went wrong and discuss how they might do better in the future.

When they do make strides in their learning, especially ones that show results such as doing their chores, or taking the time to figure out how to spend their money wisely, praise them for their smart behavior, and the success that they are building on. It helps when you make the praise specific to the accomplishment, to help it stick in their minds... "Hey, I noticed that you put extra savings aside this week..." or, "Thank you for taking out the trash, that will help add to your piggy bank funds!" If they are doing particularly well on saving for a specific item, comment on it and drop a few extra dollars into their savings to show your appreciation for a job well done.

Start Teaching Them Early

Offer suggestions but try to avoid being a nag about it. Remember... the best way to develop your child's good spending habits is to allow them to make choices. They may not always do what you want them to (even outside their spending and saving habits!), but if they are going to learn, they have to be able to make their own decisions.

You can discuss their decisions with them, but ultimately, they have to be given the right to choose for themselves. You can offer direction in little ways to encourage them to make better decisions, such as, "Here is the allowance you worked for this week... how close are you getting to that new bike you wanted?" In this way, you are offering them positive support, instead of nagging them into doing what you want them to do. It will produce much better results!

Super Savers

Good Money Manners

Manners and etiquette have always fallen upon the parents to teach their children. Having good money manners and etiquette should be no different. They need to understand, especially at a young age and they are excited to be learning about money, that it is never okay to ask someone how much money they have, or to rub it in others' faces that they have less money than you do. These are the same behaviors that will follow them through their school and adult years, so raise them in the way that makes them a positive influence, rather than a money bully.

Talk About Purchases

Having discussions with why you make the purchases you do, can help your children decide what is a good, valid purchase, and what may be a frivolous waste of money. Is there a particular reason why you buy one brand of dish soap over another? Does it make the dishes cleaner the first go around, versus a lesser brand that you may need to use twice as much to break through the grease?

If you have a coupon for an item, or something is on sale... is it really worth spending the money on, if it isn't something you would buy in the first place? Maybe it's a better brand that is now reduced to the more affordable price you are paying? These are all things that can be examined and taken into consideration when discussing why looking at the options is important when making purchases, even if something is on sale.

Defining Needs and Wants

As we discussed previously, this is an important lesson, and one that can be taught from an early age. When children understand the real difference between what they really need as opposed to getting something that they want, they learn how to make better money decisions. This is also the basis for beginning to teach your children about the concepts

Super Savers

of delayed gratification and impulse buying, two very valuable lessons.

The next time you and your children are out and about, and they ask you to buy something, start having some patient discussions with them. Is this something that they actually need, or is it something that they want? Would it be really hard for them to go without this purchase, or is it something they could live without? It can become a game between you and your children, one where they can really think about their answers, and give you their views on each item.

Financial literacy doesn't have to be hard or involved. In fact, the more fun you make it for them, the more the lessons are likely to stick. There is a game app created for the phone, *Money Mammals' Needs vs. Wants*, that can help add to the element of fun for your child as they go through the game, deciding on what are needs versus wants, when it comes to making decisions about different items. There are other games out there too, that will help make your child's journey along the path of money understanding a more fun way to learn.

From Toddler to Teen

We have an amazing opportunity to teach our children in stages as they grow, from toddler to teenager, about how to become financially responsible and how to be wise consumers. We will be going into some age-related concepts and activities later in the book, but I wanted to touch base with you here on some of the more general concepts to help your children understand, no matter the age, how their decision-making skills can always be improved upon... and why it's important to do so!

Super Savers

Consumer Wisdom

Every time your child looks to buy something new, it becomes an opportunity to teach them to become more responsible with their money. Take the time to review with them different alternatives for spending their money... need versus want, new versus used, immediate need/want versus delayed gratification... these are all good ways to help your child become better financial decision makers.

Teach them the art of comparison shopping to save money, or to review quality versus cost. Teach your kids to be commercial savvy, so that they understand the role that advertisers have, and how they try to draw you to a product for purchase, even though it may not really be the best product available. Value for price is a huge lesson for kids, and ones that they will likely enjoy learning and using as they mature.

Contentment

Of all the lessons that you can teach your children about money, contentment is right up there as one of the most powerful. This is an especially powerful lesson to bring up when your children start exhibiting attitudes of entitlement, or when they get whiny because they want something.

> *"There are two ways to be rich—one is to have everything you want, and the other is to be satisfied with what you have."*
>
> *~Unknown*

When children start exhibiting signs of wanting something, it can help to go over a list of all the things that they do have or are experiencing. It helps to put it in perspective of how much they truly have, both physical and enjoyment-wise, rather than allowing them to keep their focus on something that they may want that they don't already have. This can

Super Savers

sometimes help us to remember the blessings we enjoy.

This may often be a daily battle, but it is part of a journey of gratitude that you can continually take with your children. Rather than spending focus on what you don't have, it is a lesson in counting your blessings. It is about ceasing to compare yourself to others or to the number of things you possess as compared to someone else, and to always be grateful and to say thank you for what you do possess in life. And it is a never-ending journey of gratitude.

Keep it Simple

Let's be honest, children live far more in the now than we do as adults, and this can make them incredibly short-sighted when it comes to the bigger picture of life. When their minds can barely see past the fact that there is pizza on the school lunch menu for tomorrow, it is hard to get the concept of future anything across to them in a way that sinks in. The best way to start encouraging this view to the future is to help them to start setting goals.

Keep goals short-term to begin with. Maybe 1-2 days to start. Then stretch it to a goal that will take them a week to achieve, then 2 weeks, a month... By building this anticipation and actualization slowly, you will get them to learn that they can plan ahead to the future, and understand that the future actually does arrive, even if it takes a while. If you start with longer goals to begin the lessons, they may lose sight of the goal, and sometimes forget it all together. Take your time and build slowly. After all, we are talking about an eventual lifetime of future building and patience.

Especially in the beginning, make the goals simple and attainable to their direct wants and needs. Help them to work toward specific goals like a toy, a video game, or a trip to go get ice cream at Dairy Queen. These should not be abstract goals at the start

Super Savers

(abstract to them, such as saving for college, or a car, or moving out when they are 18). These goals hold no real sense of reality for them yet. They need the understand the concept of goals and the achievement of them, if you want them to be able to set and meet goals on their own, and for their lifetime.

Keep budgeting simple too. Don't make it about every penny at first. Make it about how much they have coming in versus how much they have going out, and how much can be put away. They need to start with the basics in order to fully grasp an understanding of how the financial system works, and how it impacts even their young lives, before moving to the more complicated aspects of budgeting and financial planning. With all lessons, starting with the basics will give them a stronger basis for understanding that they will carry into their future.

Teach Your Children to be Super Savers

There are many ways that we can reach our children and teach them how to be amazing Super Savers as they move into their financial futures. But there are a few basic things we can do, other than those we have already discussed, to keep it simple enough to help them gain the true basis for understanding that they need to eventually make these decisions on their own, without our guiding hand.

Start with Goal Setting

Like we mentioned above, start with setting goals that are simple and easy to achieve to begin with. As the goals become more complicated and take longer to achieve, children can be taught (just as we have learned as adults), that sometimes there are sacrifices that can be made to shorten your path to goal achievement.

Super Savers

Before setting a goal, sit down and have a discussion with your children about how they would like to spend the money that they earn. Let them work through the processes of short-term candy bar to long-term video game, giving them food for thought. Discuss with them the length of time it takes for them to earn the money they are receiving, and what the value is if they buy a candy bar and it's gone before you even get home, or saving for something that lasts longer, and gives them something to show for the work they have done.

It should come as no surprise that studies have shown that those who are the most successful are the people in life who set goals. This, then, becomes a habit of great importance to teach our children. It is best to help them set specific goals, but also to keep the goals realistic, to encourage their ability to achieve them and move on to set the next goal.

Explain Savings Basics

It is important to dedicate your time to teaching your children to be Super Savers instead of diehard spenders. It is natural for most children to want to take their allowance or birthday money and go off and spend it on something... anything! Spending money and buying things can be exciting for adults, as well as children.

However, if you take the time to have the proper discussions with your children, they may be very open to making their money last or sticking it away for a much larger purchase later on... the benefits of savings.

When your child does start talking about something special or cool that they really want, use that opportunity to start a discussion about saving, setting goals, and how they can achieve what they want by working towards it. You can discuss different options such as their having to save for the

Super Savers

entire amount themselves, or whether you might contribute a portion if they save a certain amount.

It is important for your kids to learn that their money carries value, and so do their purchases. There is both a short- and long-term effect to their spending and saving, and by planning, they can control the effect. Whatever it takes, work with how your child understands the concepts of saving best, so that they will be inspired to bigger and greater things in the future.

Split Funds Up

When children get funds coming in from whatever source, whether it be allowance, odd jobs, birthday money, etc., it can be a great time to sit down and talk to them about splitting up how their money is used, just like anyone would with a simple budget. Talk about splitting their money into 3 categories: one for saving, one for spending, and one for giving.

Discuss with them what each of the categories is for, and then help them decide how much they want to set aside for each category. This can be a percentage each time they earn money, or they can make a decision each time money comes in on how they want to split it up. Let them place the amounts according to importance to them, as long as they set aside money in each category. It is a simple way to start teaching budgeting skills, as well as making sure that they are always setting aside an amount for savings.

Chapter 3: Responsible Spending

There are many aspects that we can look at when we want to start talking to our children about responsible spending. Some of these are age-related… what will our children be able to understand at which age, and how can we teach it to them? Some are psychological, some are technical. How do we navigate through the very complicated world of finance in such a way that our children will be able to understand and benefit?

Quite honestly, that is going to change from one family to the next, and from one child to the next.

Super Savers

For us to have the ability as parents to teach our children, we must have our own basis of understanding first. So, this journey is not just about our children learning, in many ways, there are aspects of financial literacy that we are exploring and learning right alongside of them.

And that's okay! Take it as a point of pride that you are trying to teach your children something that will benefit them throughout their lifetime, and perhaps we need to remember to be open to the process ourselves. As they say, "It's never too late to learn."

Intentional Spending

If you have struggled throughout your life with saving and budgeting, you are not alone. There is a whole psychology of finance dedicated to the concept of "Behavioral Finance". This complicated philosophy can be broken down in part and looked at through our lens of learning intentional spending and saving.

"When it comes to saving—self-control is not a problem in the future, but a problem now. We know we should be saving—we will do it next year—but today, let's spend. This immediate gratification causes us to think about saving, but end up spending."

~ Shlomo Benartzi, American Behavioral Economist

Intentional spending, and saving, is a complicated process involving examination, delayed gratification, and opportunity cost. When we stop to focus on trying to understand our own financial behaviors… the how and why we make the decisions that we do, we need to start with our everyday financial decisions. When we break it down into its simplest form, opportunity and opportunity cost is what money is truly all about.

Super Savers

Economists are a breed of their own, as far as how they can break things down for us less savvy folk. They will tell you that it is difficult, at best, to be intentional with money whether it's for saving or spending. If these brilliant money examiners are saying it is hard, then the question becomes... How will we be able to grasp it ourselves, and how will we break it down further to teach our children?

It is here that the phrase "break it down" holds the key. When we look at how we want (or need) to spend or save, we need to break it down into smaller questions and steps, in order to maximize the benefits. This is one of the main reasons I started the Daily Dollar Finances blog and podcast (www.dailydollarfinances.com), with the primary goal of making personal finance concepts simple and actionable, one day at a time.

Balancing Intentional Spending and Saving

Good financial planning centers around the thought that you need to balance your needs and wants of today with your needs and wants of tomorrow. Your children may have several reasons that would make them want to save money. This can include a new toy or video game, a new bike, a trip somewhere special, a car, or college... whatever age they are at, and activities they enjoy, those items are going to change and switch in levels of importance to them.

It's even possible, if you began their training in finances early on, that they may be putting away money for more than one goal at a time... a shorter- and longer-term goal. But everything in moderation! However, it is possible to focus so much on what you want to save for, that you forget to enjoy your now. And that isn't something that we want to pass onto our children. It can be all too easy to become obsessed with saving because there is always something out there that we want to save for!

Super Savers

When you learn to become more intentional about your saving and spending, you start to break down your wants and needs and start asking the right questions to reach a personal determination:

- How much money are you going to need to achieve your savings goal?
- When are you going to need the money?
- Is there a way to invest the money to make it work better for reaching your goal?

It is by working through these questions with your children, that you can help them determine how much money they are going to actually need to put away into savings. If it turns out that they will need to save more money than they are currently making in order to meet their goal, that's okay! There are a couple of additional questions you can ask them to help them make their savings determinations.

- Is there a way to lower how much you actually need to save?

- Can you push back the date of the goal… when you need the money?

- Is there a way to receive a better investment return on your money?

When parents and children work on saving with intention, they have a greater opportunity to get what they want from life. However, you also need to help your children recognize that when they save with intention, they must also spend with intention.

The first question to spending with intention is simple… What makes you happy?

- Buying something special for yourself… a new book? New clothes?
- Going out and spending time with friends at the movies? Playing sports?

Super Savers

- Playing the newest video game or watching the latest movie release?

You want to discourage the answer of making lots of money and putting it away for savings. While this may seem admirable, it can develop into a money disorder known as financial hoarding, which isn't something that we really want for our children. We want them to be financially secure, while still taking the time to enjoy those things in life that they love to do.

If they don't have answers for these questions, which can happen, try rephrasing the question in a different way... what things that you bought or spent money on in the past year (or months when it comes to smaller children, because their answers frequently change with developing tastes) made you happy or excited?

Responsible Spending

Have an honest conversation with what things make them happy. Maybe talk about the things that once made them happy, that are now replaced with different things. The concept of intentional spending is the determination of what makes you the happiest or brings a sense of enjoyment, and then planning how to adjust the financial balance between saving and spending, so you can make as much of that happen as possible.

Intentional spending starts with intentional saving. Once you can help your child figure out their true goals and whether they can be adapted or adjusted, they then have an amount remaining that can be examined for intentional spending. By looking at what makes them happy, and having honest discussions about it, they can better allocate their money left over from their intentional saving for tomorrow, to focus on what makes them happiest today. The goal is to teach them how plan their finances so they can focus their spending on those

Super Savers

things that have more value to them, instead of wasting it on those things that don't.

However, if they save intentionally first, they know what they have left to spend today. Then, it's simply a matter of determining how you'll spend on this, and how much on that. The goal is to plan your finances so you can spend more on what you value and less on what you don't.

Intentional spending and saving can be hard. It involves building a habit in the way you save and spend, and as we all know, breaking and building habits takes a lot of work! This is a lesson that shouldn't be just a "one and done", it is an examination that should be on-going, helping your child to build a habit of being financially responsible.

Delayed Gratification

Delayed gratification is never an easy concept to teach children. It is often hard for adults to understand. Our society has become what can only be called a "fast food" society. We want what we want, when we want it, and often on a whim, so the "when" that we want it is now—instant gratification versus delayed gratification.

Waiting = More Appreciation

With everything coming at us, available at our fingertips within sometimes even minutes, it's no wonder that our children are growing up with the concept that if they want it, they should be able to have it right now.

We live in a world of instant gratification, one that is becoming more so all the time, and there are sadly far too many kids who grow up thinking that if they want it, they should have it right now. There is no

Super Savers

true concept of what delayed gratification is, because they have become accustomed to being rewarded for nothing, and immediately, without waiting or earning it.

When we work on the concepts of financial responsibility with our children, saving is a big part of it. Savings usually means delayed gratification, so rather than allowing our children to become accustomed to instant gratification, if we want them to become Super Savers, the concept of delayed gratification is something that needs to be instilled as soon as possible.

There is something to be said for delayed gratification, even outside of financial responsibility. When we are given something immediately, when we want it, we honestly place less value on it. It becomes just another "thing" in an endless cycle of "things". When receive something that we have worked hard for, waited for, we appreciate the value of what we get far, far more. It helps to build the appreciation of contentment, because what we have earned and waited for holds more value to us, rather than just moving onto the next thing on our endless list of wants.

Sleep on It

One of the most common recommendations made for teaching delayed gratification is the concept of "sleeping on it." This doesn't really mean to actually sleep on it, but it does mean to give your child the time to think about it overnight, or even better, for 24 hours before moving forward (or not) in making a purchase. Sometimes we get caught up in the excitement of seeing something at a store that we want, or an advertisement that displays an item that is enticing.

Of course, stores and companies spend heavily on trying to elicit that instantaneous impulse buy from you. Their ads and displays are geared to exactly

Super Savers

that. There is a reason why they put candy, magazines, and other little items up by the checkout lane. There is a whole aspect of consumerism that is specifically built around placement to encourage impulse buying.

Talk to your child and make the recommendation of waiting at least a day before making a purchase of something they want. Talk to them afterwards and see if they still want it at that point, or if they even remember it. If their desire is still there, then help them look at their budget and see whether it fits into their spending or savings budgets, and help them work out a way to get what they want, by developing a plan that is set up in a financially responsible way for them to achieve their new goal.

Purchase Timing

Most of us are aware that there are better times of the year to make certain purchases if we want to get the best new products, or the best price on others.

By understanding these cycles, and helping your children to understand them as well, you not only encourage tendencies toward delayed gratification, but help them to better understand how timing a purchase can play a role in any market you look at.

You can find guides to these purchases if you look online. Here is a little guidance on some items that children commonly purchase and/or save towards, with explanations that you can share with your children, to help them better understand the "why" that delayed gratification can be important.

Video Games: January

Most video game companies put out large quantities of games throughout the fall, gearing up for Christmas sales. This leaves January as the best time to purchase video games, when they usually hit the best sales after the Christmas rush is over.

Super Savers

Cell Phones: February

It may seem like an odd time for cell phone sales to pop up, but because of Valentine's Day, you can often find "Buy One Get One Free" sales, to promote communications between loved ones.

Chocolate: March

For the same reason, Valentine's Day, an extra amount of chocolate is created. These sales become the best after this holiday, and even better yet going into March. Because everyone is indulging in the sales that leftover Valentine's Day chocolates provide, other chocolate comes down in price around this time too.

Sneakers: April

As the weather starts to warm up, companies that produce sneakers promote additional sales because they know it can take just a little push to convince people that this is the time to start dedicating to working out before the summer hits.

Desks: May

A lot of new businesses start up following Tax Day (April 15th). Companies gear up their sales of office furniture and supplies with this cyclical trend being noted.

Gym & Sports Equipment: June

By this time, many people have forgotten or let go of their New Years' resolutions, so gyms and activity sellers launch sales to help move inventory.

Video Games: July

Yes... video games have 2 popular selling times throughout the year, when you can get the best prices. This is the best time especially for video console games, with sales a few months after the games have initially been released. PC gamers can also take advantage of video game sales like Steam's Summer Sale.

Super Savers

Clothing & School Supplies: August

This is the time of the year for big sales on back-to-school clothing and school supplies. Not only do huge sales abound, but many states also offer reduced or zero sales tax on these items when bought between a particular time frame.

Bicycles: September

Ironically, with bicycles, the newest models tend to be released around the end of the traditional riding season. This is a great time to find deals on last year's models.

Jeans: October

Jeans are typically the most common leftover item from all of the back-to-school sales. It is best to buy them between back-to-school and the upcoming holiday if you want to cash in on the best possible sales.

Responsible Spending

Candy: November

After Halloween candy sales are common during this time, and the cuts to cost can be enormous. The stores want to move this candy out so they can bring the Christmas candy in!

Televisions & Other Electronics: December

These sales usually tend to continue past Black Friday and Cyber Monday, pushing all the way through to the Super Bowl!

Paying Cash Not Credit

Plastic has become a major thing in our society. Even our "cash" purchases are often made using a debit card. Most children don't understand the difference between debit and credit cards. The lack of actual, physical money makes finances far more abstract for them. In order to teach them properly, we may need to start with using a physical cash system, and then move on to explaining the

Super Savers

differences between a debit card being a form of cash, where a credit card is something that can get you in trouble if not handled wisely.

Credit cards have risen to the forefront of today's financial system, greatly due to our instant gratification mentalities. We have started to make our purchases with credit, when we don't have the cash, so that we can have what we want right now. This is a place where you really need to take care to teach by example. If your children watch you continue to buy whatever you want, regardless of having the money available to pay for it, anything you try to teach them about the warnings of using credit aren't going to carry you very far.

The goal is to teach your children how to be financial Super Savers, and how to be able to manage a workable budget. To do this, a better way might be using a cash budget system to teach them, and to avoid discussions of credit until later. It is about teaching them how to save for what they want, instead of falling prey to the lure of the instant gratification that credit can bring… along with all the headaches that go with it.

As your kids hit that magical age of 18, they are going to be hounded by credit card companies and offers of loans to secure them what they want in the present, instead of preparing for their future. If you haven't worked out with them the lessons of why incurring debt can be very bad for their financial stability, you leave them open to becoming just another credit card victim.

It isn't that having a little debt is the end of ever becoming financially stable or successful, but there is a need to teach our children how to borrow in a responsible way. It is a complicated topic, but you can work with your child to learn the ins and outs of what debt means and how it can be handled responsibly. After all, there are very few adults who

Super Savers

get away without ever having incurred debt at one point of their lives or another. Prepare them for the eventuality of it happening in theirs, and it will benefit them throughout their lives.

When you feel comfortable talking with your children about it, sit them down and discuss how having incurred debt has affected your life. Discuss how you borrow money, and under what circumstances it may be necessary. Do you have a house payment? A car loan? What does having a loan mean? What does it make you responsible for? What happens if the loan goes into default?

If your child has a larger purchase they want, such as a computer, video game console, or a bike, offer to give them a loan for it. Make them earn at least half of it first, so that they have a suitable down payment. Do the research with them to compare costs or find a sale if possible.

Responsible Spending

Offer to let them repay the amount you are loaning them in weekly or monthly payments. Actually work out a payment schedule with them, and charge them a "convenience fee", much like an interest fee, over and above the amount that they borrow. Your child should come out of the lesson learning about loans and interest, and how it can affect other things they may want in the future, during their repayment of the loan. In this way, they can learn to have a healthy attitude about credit.

Chapter 4: Paying It Forward

We touched upon the need to separate out your children's financial responsibilities into saving, spending, and into giving. There are many financial sites that talk about the need for our children to learn the art of giving when it comes to their personal finances. Few of them go into what the true benefits are for teaching your child about charitable giving.

Why Giving is Important

The most common way in teaching our children about financial responsibility is to show them how

Super Savers

to set a budget and separate out their received funds into four categories: spending, saving, investing, and giving. They even have partitioned piggy banks available, already split into these categories. The reasons are more obvious when it comes to savings, spending, and investing. But why is giving to others such an important component and valuable lesson in financial responsibility?

Most parents tend to focus on the other three aspects of financial responsibility. Not all of them agree with the importance of charitable giving. This is very sad, because such giving, and helping our children to partake in it, has so much more to teach them than just the giving of our money to others now and then. It develops certain life skills for them that are harder to teach in other ways.

Empathy

We all have a certain degree of empathy with which we are born. But to really bring out the best of our empathic abilities, we must nurture the trait. Doing so creates a beneficial level of social consciousness and awareness, making the world a far better place when we feel empathy for those who are less fortunate than we are, and do something to act upon our empathic feelings.

When we teach our children about giving to those in need, we are also teaching them that every little thing we do can have an impact on the lives of others. By starting at a young age, it can have a beneficial impact because it shows them that even their contributions, as a small child, can work to make a difference in others' lives.

We don't want our children to go through personal or physical tragedy before they understand the capacity and need to have compassion for others. Sometimes that is what it takes for people to reach a true place of compassion. In reality, compassion and

Super Savers

empathy can be cultivated early on, and will guide them toward being better people.

Some careers usually have people with strong tendencies of having empathy for others. Nurses, doctors, psychiatrists, psychologists, and the like, are all career choices that are in high demand and mostly pay good salaries. When empathy is nurtured, these are respectable career opportunities that may be available down the road for your child.

Gratitude

Charity work can also instill a sense of gratitude in your child, that helps lead them down the road of contentment, a valuable commodity when one is looking to be financially responsible. The experience of charitable giving of their time and/or their money exposes your children to the concept of diversity of both people and life experiences.

Gratitude starts to give them the understanding that no matter what happens in life, there will always be someone less fortunate. This helps your child with the concept that they will always have something in life to be grateful for. When children truly learn the lessons of gratitude and contentment, they are less likely to fall into the trap of consumerism debt like so many others.

Encouragement of Passions

When you are first sitting down to talk to your kids about what kind of charitable organization they might possibly want to involve themselves in, it can help to try and steer them toward something they already have a passion for. If they like to read, donating money or books to those charities that work with reading literacy might be an idea. When children love something, they gain a sense of pride being a part of it, even in such a way as contributing to a charity that might represent those passions.

Super Savers

The opposite can be true too. If they choose a charity that "sounds good" to them in the moment, they may find themselves developing a passion in that direction. Many people who donate to animal charities find enjoyment with working with animals. Who knows? It may lead your child toward becoming a veterinarian.

Basic Money Management

Not only does charitable giving help to teach your children the basics of money management but it also focuses on the basics of simple mathematics as well. Breaking their income down into percentages for each account category, including giving, teaches them a skill in money management that will last them their entire life.

It also lends to learning simple mathematic basics such as fractions, percentages, and decimals. When they can do this through the physical handling of their money, it helps to make the lesson even stronger, to stick with them. It helps them to break it down, figure out how much goes into each of their accounts, and encourages them to do the necessary math to make it all happen.

College Applications

The other added benefit of charitable giving is that this is something that many higher end colleges look for in their application approval process. Whether the charity work your child does is invested in time or money, colleges look for evidence of philanthropy on the applications for their perspective students. The longer your child has been involved in charitable giving, the better it looks for the application. This is something your child can get excited about to be able to list on their application, and it will appear less last-minute or contrived to the college admissions board.

Super Savers

Soft Skills

Soft skills are those skills in life that don't have a measurable value but are often some of the most valuable skills of all when it comes to character development and who you turn out to be as a person. Empathy is one of those. So is the integrity and social responsibility that they gain when they learn to connect with and help those in need. This is something that teaches them the valuable lesson in becoming both respectable and honorable as they grow into their amazing potential as adults. It also helps to give them a greater sense of purpose as individuals... true financial superheroes.

The Act of Giving

The act of giving is a powerful life lesson that can be learned at any age. When you do sit down and talk to your child about giving to charity, you can also discuss with them the different options that they have for giving. Donation does not just have to be about money.

You can talk to them about making gifts, such as crocheting or knitting hats for those going through chemotherapy. Or they can donate time to helping others in need. Discussing the various options and helping them decide how they want to get involved, and on what level, teaches your children valuable lessons in exploring options, being resourceful, and that time can be equivalent to money.

Chapter 5: Supercharge Their Savings

When we talk about supercharging your child's savings, it's not only financial considerations that come into play. It is also about supercharging their interest in saving money and learning how to budget appropriately. There are a few steps that you can take to help supercharge both their interest, and their savings, to get them started on the right path to becoming a Super Saver.

Super Savers

Compounding Interest

This is a difficult concept to teach adults, let alone to help our children understand, and yet it can be a very valuable lesson for making the most of your savings. The concept that their money can earn interest is a start, but then add to the mix that their interest can earn interest and it gets a little trickier.

The lesson started with the charitable concept of time having a value that can be equated to money. We've also talked about teaching your children the value of delayed gratification, which also relates to time. I'm not saying that compound interest relates to time in the same way, but if children have been learning these other lessons about how time and money interact, it can make it easier to take the discussion of how time can add value to money to the next level.

Explain Interest

If we want our children to grasp the concept of compound interest, we first must explain what interest is. If you did the exercise with them on loans, having them pay a set amount extra for the money that they borrow from, then they should understand how interest can affect them financially in a negative way. Now it's time to show them how interest can work to their financial benefit.

How you tackle your approach to teaching your kids about interest is going to be dependent upon their age and level of understanding. Either way, it will benefit them if you keep it simple, and expand upon their knowledge as they start to understand more and more. The first step can be as simple as… banks pay you interest to keep your money there, with them. The longer your money stays with them, the more interest you earn, thus the more money you make.

Super Savers

Work with your child to get them thinking about the concept of interest. Try a simple exercise. If they could have $10,000 right now, or a penny in the bank, which would they choose? Most children will choose the larger amount of $10,000.

Now explain to them that the interest on the penny, in this case, would be to double the amount in the bank every day that it is in the bank. So, the first day you would have $.01. Day 2, you would have $.02, Day 3, you would have $.04... and so on. Which would they choose then? Since most children don't do the projection math in their heads, they will be most likely to still choose the $10,000.

From there you can show them the math of what it would look like if the account started with that single penny doubled in daily value. By the time you reach 30 days, the account would be worth over $5.3 million. A single day later, day 31, it would be worth over $10 million. Of course, this isn't the type of interest they can expect to receive on their real-world savings or investment accounts, but it does help to illustrate the point of compound interest.

Then again, it also helps to go back and point out that if they have a loan and are paying compound interest, that can work against them financially. It works with other bills too. If bills are not paid on time, they accrue interest, or late fees, which can add up quickly. This means that the amount that they owe can add up quickly, affect their credit, and often even affect their ability to pay, if they let it go too far.

Even young children can grasp the concept of interest if you explain it to them properly. You can take the simple loan example, where you offer to loan them $5. Tell them they will be expected to pay it back the following week, only instead of paying back the $5, they will have to pay you an additional $.25, just for the convenience of being able to use the money right away, instead of waiting. If they don't

Super Savers

pay the full amount back the following week, another $.25 will be added onto the amount. It is a quick and easy lesson on how fast the interest can add up, especially if they don't earn enough in a week to pay off the full amount.

With smaller children especially, again, it helps to have visual aids, so they can better understand the concepts of what you are trying to teach them. For instance, you might teach them about interest by having them put a penny in a glass jar every day. Every other day, you can add a penny into the jar alongside of them as "interest" on the funds that the child is putting into savings.

Draw lines on the jar to show that when they reach a certain amount, their money will start earning more, because there is more in the savings. Eventually, when it reaches the first line, you might start adding a nickel instead, and then at the second line, a dime. As long as the money stays in the jar, and is at the level that warrants it, they receive the higher interest.

If they take money out and it falls below the "dime line", they go back to only getting a nickel. This teaches them that they can choose to leave their money in savings and watch it grow, or they can take it out and start all over, or at a lesser rate of interest. This helps them to learn to make sound financial choices and decisions, based on what they want or need.

Teaching Compound Interest

Start with a toy or other item that your child really wants. Discuss with them how much the item costs, and how much they make or earn from chores, etc. You can tell them that they can buy the toy when they have the money. Offer to set up an account for them to achieve their goal faster, by giving them compound interest on the money that they earn and save.

Super Savers

Set the amount of compound interest that you are willing to pay weekly (or daily, if you wish) on the money that they earn and save. Some suggested amounts may be 3%, 5%, or even 10%. Create a chart on the wall to mark their progress and to show how much money goes in and out of savings (if they pull money out for something else), and to show how compound interest amounts going in are affected by the amount of money that is in the account. The longer they leave the money in the account without touching it, the faster they will see that they will reach their goal.

Make sure to mark their progress clearly, maybe at the end of each week, or even at the end of each month, depending on how big the item they are saving for, and the amount they are able to set aside to go into savings.

Keep it Real

When you are using these higher interest amounts to demonstrate to your children about how compound interest works (or even simple interest), make sure to be clear that these are not the rates that they will find in the real world when they venture outside your walls financially. The rates that they are going to receive from an actual bank are not going to be as high as they are getting in their demonstration.

However, we do want to keep the encouragement high for their savings goals throughout their lives. It helps to get them excited about it, and yet we need to make sure they understand the reality of it in the real world. The reason to work with them on the levels we do when teaching them, is that it takes a great deal of money to see any true rewards coming from interest accrual when we are saving.

But we want them to get excited about it now, even when they only have $5 to put aside. This

Super Savers

excitement, and teaching them how to manage their money and savings when they are young and the stakes are far lower, is what will carry through as a positive habit when they are older and they are actually able to deposit real paychecks into their bank accounts to start earning interest.

Gifting for a Head Start

There are several methods that you can use to give your child a head start when it comes to readying them financially for their future. One way that they can be helped is through opening a 529 Plan for them. It is a gift of college tuition and giving them a head start at coming out of college debt-free. As we know, going to college is your child's best shot at having a chance to compete in today's work market. This is one of the greatest financial gifts that you can give them.

If you have looked at the amount of money that is going to be needed for your child to get through any collegiate level degree program, the you know that it is a considerable amount. In an annual survey by *U.S. News*, reported data for the 2019-2020 school years showed annual college tuition levels at $41,426 for private colleges, $11,260 for public colleges if you are a state resident, and $27,120 for public colleges if you are from out-of-state.

That does not even include the peripherals needed, such as books, living expenses, and other fees. Over the course of a several year degree program, this can add up to a small fortune! This is why so many college students graduate with a large student loan debt to begin their lives, because of the amount of money they have to borrow, just to make a good education happen.

When you give your child a head start by giving them the ability to start their graduated life free of debt, or

Super Savers

with low debt incurred, this is a significant contribution to their future. They will be able to save more of their take home paycheck, buy a home at a much earlier age, or even start a business, which is how many Americans find their own path to financial success.

Even the experts say that one of the best ways to help your child prepare for their educational future is to save through a 529 plan. The money that you set aside to grow for them is tax free, and as long as the money is used to pay for college-related expenses, you will not even have to pay taxes on the assets of the account when they are used or sold.

A 529 plan has no restrictions on income and can be set up by anyone for your child. This means that parents, grandparents, family friends, or any other relative can set up a 529 savings plan for your child.

Supercharge Their Savings

A Roth IRA Account

This is another option to help contribute a financial gift to your child's future. This is an extremely effective financial way to help your child get a running head start on investing for retirement. Contributions to a Roth IRA are paid in after-tax dollars, which means that any gains in the account accumulate tax-free.

If you start this for your child, or grandchild, when they are still very young, it is a remarkable opportunity. Decades of tax-free growth can be accumulated. The only real stipulation is that your child must have some form of earned income in order for them to have a Roth IRA opened for them.

This is a benefit to consider when your child first starts earning money that produces a W-2 form. Although, if there is a way to document their earnings through an independent contractor 1099

Super Savers

form instead of a standard wage earned w-2, that is acceptable too. To give you an example…

If your teenager, at 16, invests $4,800 annually ($400 a month) into their Roth IRA, by the time he or she reaches the age of 60, there will be $2,405,162 available for them, assuming they got an average 9% rate of return. Of that total balance, $211,200 came from the contributions of your child, while the remaining $2,193,962 are investment gains. Taxable under most other investment accounts, using a Roth IRA this is all considered tax-free money.

They can even start their Roth IRA once they start earning income from other sources, such as babysitting and odd and end jobs. They just need to show earned income in order to get started. They can contribute any amount to their Roth IRA on a weekly or monthly basis, as long as they do not exceed the lesser of either their full earned income amount, or the maximum allowed for that year, which is $6,000 as of 2020.

Age is not a consideration, as long as they have the earned income for contribution. Even a 2-year-old paid for being in a commercial can contribute their earned income to a Roth IRA. A parent can open a custodial account for any children under the age of 18 and manage the contributed funds until the child reaches 18 (or 21 in some states). Several brokerages such as Fidelity or Charles Schwab offer these types of accounts.

Matching Contributions

Matching contributions is a great way to give your child a head start toward becoming a Super Saver. However, the first thing you need to think very strongly upon… don't use what would go into your own retirement in order to benefit your children's retirement or other funding/saving needs. Instead

Super Savers

of helping them, in the long run, you might be creating a situation where you will be reliant upon them to take care of you, when the goal is to make them self-sufficient enough not to need the help of others for their own financial survival.

Matching contributions can be handled in a number of ways. You can work with your children to match any funds that they put away into their savings, either starting at a certain amount, or up to a certain amount. This can be done from the time they start saving pennies away in a jar at the age of 3. Or you can offer to match a percentage of what they put away from their paycheck as a teen, such as 10%, giving them a boost to their savings. You can offer to increase that amount once their account reaches, and stays above, a certain level. In this way, you are continually encouraging them to keep their money in savings in order to achieve a greater benefit.

Supercharge Their Savings

You can also offer to match a certain amount that they specifically set aside for college, or for an IRA or other investment option that they choose (which we will be looking at in the next chapter). The point of matching funds is not only to give your child a boost towards their savings goals, but also you are sending them a message that you believe in their ability to grow and responsibly handle their financial future. You are telling them, even without words, that you believe that they can become a financial superhero, and that you want to be a part of their life to watch them grow and succeed.

Chapter 6: Going Beyond the Piggy Bank

One of the steps you can take to bring your child to the status of financial superhero, is to talk with them about investing. Once they have started to get the hang of what money is, how it works (and can work for them), among other financial concepts, now comes the time to ready them with the valuable tool of long-term investing, preparing them for a lifetime of financial stability and responsibility.

Of course, children are going to learn and mature at different rates. It may be a while before they are

Super Savers

ready to jump into the world of learning about asset allocation and portfolio creation. You can start teaching most children at least the basic concept of investing while they are still young.

Risk vs. Reward

Risk versus reward is one of the beginning initial concepts that you can help your child to learn about at a very young age and is pretty much the basis for being able to make sound investment choices in their future. Reward may be something they already understand, if you have started working with them about interest, money management, savings, etc. Risk is the other side of the coin, one that isn't usually covered in the traditional financial conversation surrounding earning and saving. Risk is a possibility that your investment can potentially lose part, or even all, of its value.

Gain Their Interest

You can begin your child's education into investing by showing them the stocks and other investment vehicles that you own. This can really draw their attention if your stocks are something that they can relate to, such as a technology company like Apple or a social media company like Facebook or a manufacturer such as Nike. It could also be a retail giant like Wal-Mart or Target or even a media company like Disney. These are all concepts that may get your child's attention and thus may increase their interest.

Next, show your child the company's investor's relations page, and talk with them about the information that is displayed. Show them where to look to find how much a company has earned, how many people they employ, and what products they make. Talk with your child about the type of companies that they like or are interested in, and which ones they can imagine themselves buying

Super Savers

stock for in the future. Let's face it, if your children are like most, don't be surprised to get the answers such as Disney, Google or Amazon.

At this point, even if they are ready to go no further, let them pick out a stock. Discuss with them the pros and cons that you can see with their choices. If that is the stock they are set on, then actually try and buy a single share (or a fractional share) for them. Afterwards, sit down with your child at least once a week and go over how the stock performed.

Show them how to watch for the rise and fall in price. Track it with them on paper so they can see how the change can happen. If you don't have the money to purchase the stock for them, then still let them pick one out, and track it together, so they can see for themselves how the fluctuations in the stock market can affect their investment.

If you start this process with them when they are young, they will learn to track the cycles as they grow and mature into their financial responsibility. Patterns are easy for children to grasp, and they might amaze you when they catch something that your adult eyes might have otherwise overlooked. The whole process, even if you are making a game of it, helps them to learn about how the market fluctuates, and can prepare them to become better decisions makers as they grow and mature.

When they become even older and are earning enough money, you may want to help them split their earnings so they can invest part of it. In this way, they can start buying their own stocks. They may lose money with some of the choices they make, but this is all part of the lesson when it comes to risk versus reward, and it will help them to watch for ways to improve their decision making when it comes to picking investments.

Super Savers

It also teaches them to review the advantages and disadvantages between their savings and investment accounts, and they may want to adjust the amounts they put into each. Whatever choices they make, they will learn how their decisions affect the amounts they earn and have to spend or save. It is a valuable lesson, whether they actually gain or lose money.

Giving Money a Job

Another way to approach your children about the idea of investing is to explain to them that what they are doing is giving their money a job. Their money goes to work in the form of an investment vehicle... stocks, bonds, money market accounts, etc. Although sometimes they lose money for their work instead of always earning.

The interest rate, or dividends, earned on their money is what drives how much they can potentially earn, or what their money can earn for them. One of the first things you can look at with your children, when trying to help them determine how best their money can work for them, is to examine the potential earnings from investment dividends versus the interest that their money will more safely earn if sitting in a bank.

Yes, a high-yield savings account with a bank will most certainly earn them the safe bet, without the risk of loss. However, there are greater potential earnings to be gained by putting their money into an investment account as shares of a stock or bond and its dividends. Sit down with your children and examine the difference between the amount of interest their money will earn from a savings account versus the potential amount their money can earn through stock purchases, or another investment vehicle.

Because interest rates for savings accounts typically run so low, it can be more difficult to show children

Super Savers

that a savings account is a good, solid vehicle with which they can grow their money. This isn't necessarily a bad thing. Banks are a good option for when you are first starting out, to learn how to become more financially responsible for managing your money. But it's not a long-term vehicle for turning your savings into wealth.

One of the benefits that children have when it comes to investing, is that they have a long-term horizon to let their investment choices play out. This means that they have the chance to let the stock sit and earn, maybe lose a little, and then bounce back over the course of the 50+ investment years they have ahead of them. They also have the opportunity, with this long-term view in front of them, to watch how other choices play out, and switch their investment to another form if they decide they can earn a better return that way.

Going Beyond the Piggy Bank

Choose the Type of Account

There are so many options available to you and your child as to what kind of account to set up when first starting to invest. One thing you might consider is to find a broker to help explain the options available. If you go this route, try to find one that charges no account set-up fees and has no minimum on the initial deposit.

Another consideration is how your child chooses to pursue investments. If they are looking to work with the practice of trading stocks, you may want to make sure that the broker charges low, or even no commissions on trades. If your child wants to work more in a hands-off fashion, you may want to find a broker who has a larger selection of low-cost index funds or Exchange-Traded Funds (ETFs) available.

In this way, your child isn't under any pressure to come up with additional funds if the account broker isn't properly doing their job. They can work with

Super Savers

small investments until they feel comfortable enough to try for larger ones.

In any case, what type of investment vehicle your child chooses can depend on whether or not they have earned income. A Roth IRA account, as we discussed before, is a great way to start an investment portfolio if a child has started earning wages already. As previously mentioned, its tax-free earnings remain tax and penalty free as long as the money is only pulled out under certain conditions, such as at the age of 59 ½ or later, but also a portion can be used for first home purchases, or even for education.

Another option, if your child doesn't have earned income, is a custodial brokerage account. The Uniform Gift to Minors Act or the Uniform Transfer to Minors Act allow for you to open an account for your child. The account initially starts out in your name, but dependent upon state laws, your child will be able to take over the account for themselves when they reach either 18 or 21.

Opening an Account

Depending on the type of account you and your child decide to open, it can be a lengthier process, or it could take just a few minutes. Custodial accounts for either a Roth IRA or a standard broker account can take as little as 15 minutes. For many brokers, you can complete the entire process online.

Be ready with the information you will need. The broker will likely ask for the social security numbers for both yourself and your child, along with your dates of birth, and of course, contact information. You may have to supply employment information. It is also possible that you will need to link to another account, such as a bank account, to transfer funds to the actual account you are opening.

Super Savers

Choose Investments

Once the account is open and funds have been transferred, you're all set to start the investment process. Through the brokerage account, your child will now have the option to invest in a few options... stocks, mutual funds, exchange-traded funds, and index funds. A two-step investment process may be the best vehicle for teaching your child the different options they have available to them. It keeps the lesson simple, and is easier for them to track, especially when they are first learning.

Try starting with a few stock picks first. It can help to get them more excited if you focus on names that they may be more familiar with, such as Disney, Microsoft, Apple, Hershey's, or the like. Kids tend to be more open to acceptance of those names that they already know and love.

Next, try putting the rest of the child's investment portfolio into something along the lines of low-cost index funds or ETFs. This will bring a level of diversification to your child's portfolio, because it offers the pooling of hundreds (or thousands) of other stocks into one single fund. It allows your child to invest in a larger number of companies at once, and hopefully bring them a better result long term.

As with every other lesson, sit down with your child regularly and examine how their portfolio is growing. Show them how the stocks fluctuate and change with the rises and dips in the market. Let them see for themselves how their money is working for them. Watch for both short- and long-term fluctuations to help them understand the differences in how the markets work. This can help develop on-going discussions about their finances, and how they can develop a future for themselves by staying informed.

Super Savers

Bonds

Bonds are another investment vehicle that you may want to explore with your child. Like bank savings accounts, they tend to be more low-risk, with a low-return on investment. However, they typically pay a little higher than whatever the going Prime Interest Rate is. Unlike stocks, they are usually backed by stable institutions such as governments or banks. There are lower-rated bonds that may offer better returns, but they can't always be counted on to produce the income when you are expecting it.

Bonds tend to be a little more complex, and it may be better just to start working with a stock portfolio first, and then move into bonds later in the child's investment learning.

The market can always seem a little scary, and confusing. By starting to work with your child in the market while they are young, you are making it less confusing and more accessible for them to pursue in their future. As you are going through the examination of their portfolio, keep the concepts of profit and loss and risk versus reward in the front of discussions, so you can provide clear answers to the questions that arise when the market goes through its normal fluctuations.

As your child grows older, and their understanding shows itself, encourage them to try other investment vehicles, so that they can learn what they do, and be confident of the decisions they make for their financial future.

Chapter 7: Money Lessons by Age

We've discussed a fair amount of lessons and examples that can be used to teach children how to grow into responsible financial planners. Some are straight forward, and easy to teach, while others are a little more complicated, and would be better served later in the learning process, once they have some more experience and knowledge under their belts.

Although every child is different, here are some key goals to take into consideration when starting to teach your child to be a Super Saver:

Super Savers

- **Ages 3-5**: Develop and teach key skills needed, such as planning, and multi-tasking.

- **Ages 6-12**: Work on building good money habits, behaviors, and values.

- **Ages 13-21**: Work with practicing financial skills and decision-making.

Teaching to the Learning Curve

Beth Kobliner, an American Financial commentator, has stated that as young as 3 years old, children can start to understand spending and savings as financial concepts. The *United Kingdom's Money Advice Service* commissioned research done at the University of Cambridge, who reported that by the age of 7, children's money habits were already formed.

What does this mean for the prospects of us, as parents, to teach our children about financial responsibility? We should begin at the earliest possible time to pursue every teachable moment we

Money Lessons by Age

have in order to instill in our children the ability to be Super Savers. It is to us that our children look for answers, and we hold the strongest influence on their financial behaviors. We are the ones responsible for raising our next generation to be brilliant savers, investors, consumers, and givers.

One of the first ways we do this is to teach our children how to separate their finances out and manage them, deciding what will go where. This can be done through a divided piggy bank or jar system, as we mentioned before, or else we can use envelopes as a tool for teaching money management and assignment. It is important to get our children to understand, that if they don't manage their money properly, and tell it where to go, that it will eventually go away, most often through frivolous spending without thought to the future.

These are the simplest concepts to teach children at an early age about financial management. By the

Super Savers

time our children grow into their teenage years, we should already be giving them far more responsibility over the management of their money. Teens should already be able to identify what their main expenses are, from needs such as food and clothing, through wants, such as entertainment and other activities. They should understand the concept of saving to cover needs and wants as they occur. They should grasp how to create and work within a simple budget to make sure that their spending is not exceeding their income. We do this all by gradually training them in the ways of becoming financial superheroes.

"Age appropriate" is a guideline, not a hard rule. You will be able to tell when your child is ready for the next stage of learning, or whether they may have to continue in the same lesson for a while. There is no right or wrong age, only whether or not your child understands what you are trying to teach them. Please keep this in mind when applying the guidelines below to your own child's financial training.

Ages 3-5

Things Cost Money

Teach your children that things they want and need actually cost money. This means more than just telling them, "That toy costs $5." If this is something your child wants to buy, help them figure out the cost, and then take the money out of their jar, or piggy bank funds available for spending. Then bring them to the store and let them be the one to physically hand the money to the cashier. It will have a far longer lasting impression on them as to the value of money.

Learn to Wait

We have discussed the concept of teaching our children delayed gratification. There are ways to get

Super Savers

this across, even at this young of an age. We can begin this lesson even before we begin teaching our children about money.

When you go to the park or playground, and your child gets excited about swinging, but there are no swings available and they have to stand in line, it is the perfect opportunity to start discussions about the value and need of waiting. In the wait, they are able to get something valuable... their turn to ride on the swing. If they don't want to wait and instead go play on the monkey bars, you can ask if they are just settling for something less than what they really want? Or is it worth waiting in line to get what they actually want?

This, of course, applies then to those things they want to have or buy. The ability of a child to learn the concept of delayed gratification can be a predictor as to how successful they will be when they grow to adulthood. If they learn how to delay the impulse buy until they have the cash saved up, they will be less likely to fall into credit card debt.

Other lessons can be taught at this age too, as far as delayed gratification. When you go to the store to buy something, and your child sees something that he or she wants to buy, it is a good time to turn and say, "Right now, we are here to buy *xyz*. We will make a plan to come to the store to buy what you need another time." This teaches them that they will not always get something when you go to the store. Sometimes it is not about them. There can be focus on other things.

Managing Money

This is also an age where you can begin the very basics of financial management, such as starting the 3-jar saving, spending, and giving system. You may have to wait a little before starting the investing jar, or you can have them start it now and watch the funds pile up for future investment, and tell them

Super Savers

that you are going to do something fun with them down the line with that jar.

When they receive their chore money, allow them to separate it themselves, physically, into each jar. It teaches them about separating out finances for different things, and they will have fun doing it.

This is also a time where you can start talking to them about the savings jar and implementing some of the ideas given previously in the book, allowing them to pick something they want to save for and then work to make their money grow until they can make the purchase themselves. Each time your child adds money to the savings jar, help them to count how much they have, and how much more they will need to reach their goal. You can also help them figure out how long it is going to take to reach their goal each time, to keep the thought and excitement fresh in their mind.

Money Lessons by Age

Ages 6-10

This is a good time to help your child learn how to make choices when it comes to spending money. They can start to grasp the concept that there is not an infinite amount of money available, and they have to make good choices in order to get the most from their money. They can understand that once the money is gone, there is no more left to spend.

It can be good at this age to keep up with the jars and the concept of splitting their money into appropriate amounts for each. But it is also a good time to start letting them have more involvement in making financial decisions as to how the money is spent or allocated.

You can start talking to your child about the decisions you make and why you make them. This can be something as simple as why you choose to buy generic hot dogs instead of name brand. "They

Super Savers

cost $.60 less and still taste the same." Or perhaps discuss buying things in larger quantities that you know you're going to use, because of the price break you get.

You can give your child some money, say $2-3, and let them buy fruit, giving them parameters to work with, and allow them to make the best decision for the money that they must spend. This gives them experience in being able to make choices with how they spend money.

When you're out shopping with your child, talk about the financial decisions you are asking yourself, such as, "Can I get this for cheaper somewhere else?", "I think this other store has them on sale where I can buy one, get one free," or "Is this something we really need this week?" It will help your child to understand the inner dialog that you have when trying to make decisions regarding your purchases. Children pick up on this fairly quickly at this age, and it won't be long before they will be expressing these same questions back at you.

You can also sit your child down at this age and let them understand the concept of household expenses. Work with them to create a list of what is coming in, and what is going out, and then explain to them why you manage the expenses in the way that you do.

Ages 11-13

This is the age where you can work toward your child's understanding of interest, or even compound interest. It is the time to bring home the point that the sooner they start saving, the faster their money will grow into something more tangible, due to compound interest.

This is when we can start shifting our children's focus from short term goals to long term ones. You

Super Savers

can discuss with them the difference between what they will have saved and accrued if they start now, as opposed to starting later. If they put $100 into savings every year starting at age 14, by the time they turn 65, they will have $43,598. But if they wait until they turn 35 to start saving, by the time they turn 65, they will have only saved $9,446. Both examples assume a 7% rate of return. These types of scenarios can be understood at this age range, and it teaches them valuable lessons in financial planning.

On the site www.Investor.gov, under "Financial Tools & Calculators", they have a compound interest calculator. Let your child work through some numbers, based on what they are currently earning and setting aside, so they can determine how much money they will have and by what time, if they invest a certain amount at a certain rate of interest. They can play with the calculator and keep running numbers so that they can get an understanding of how compound interest can grow their financial base.

Ages 14-18

This is a good age to have discussions about the cost of college education, and what it is going to take to get your child there. Look and compare various schools and examine the costs of what they are going to need if they choose each school. Don't let them get discouraged by the cost. You can also explain the wage difference they will experience in the job market between college and non-college educated workers, which can make it a good return on the investment.

Look to find colleges that have generous financial aid and scholarship packages, as going to college doesn't always mean having to use your own funds to pay for it. Talk to them about the difference between getting grants for school, or the need to take

Super Savers

out student loans, and how that can affect their financial future. Examine what your child would like to go to school for, the average wages they can expect to receive when they graduate, and the cost of what it's going to take to get them through it.

This can create a determination of cost versus value for the child, leading to the same lesson in other aspects of their lives. It also shows how to determine return on investment, and whether it would be worth it, or perhaps they may want to change options to make it more financially supportive to their future.

Ages 18+

This is when the harder lessons of teaching your child credit responsibility should come in. When they turn 18, they will be inundated with credit card and loan offers, and they need to think responsibly in order to not damage their financial future. Talk to them about building credit for their future as well.

Credit cards can be a useful tool to help build your credit, provided you only use them when you know you can pay the balance off the card in full for each month. Not paying it off, and especially, if they get behind, can actually cause damage to their credit future, and restrict their ability to get the funds needed when they go to buy larger ticket items such as a car or a home.

If you want to help your child find a good credit card to start building credit, show them how to find (and sit down and do the research with them) those cards that are low interest with no monthly fee. Talk to them about the importance of not using it for every day purchases, but to keep it available for times of emergency, and it is best to know that it can be paid off quickly, if not immediately, before interest starts building.

Super Savers

Contentment should be taught at an even younger age, but this is a good time to bring home the lesson, so that they will appreciate more what they do have, and not go into debt for those things they want. It is also a good time to go back over the lessons on savings, by helping them get started with their own high-yield savings account at a bank and let them develop a simple budget to work with.

You can also help them to find a part time job that will help them develop a bigger working budget. Let them make their own mistakes when it comes to money, and don't be an, "I told you so" parent. If they have gotten in a bind with their budget, help them to walk through where they went wrong with their management of it.

Their teenage years are also a great time to start teaching them the art of negotiation. When your child has hit the point where they are looking to buy bigger things, or put extra money away for something special, and they come to you to discuss it, allow them to renegotiate the rate of their allowance or what they are getting paid to do chores. This will serve them well when they start working in the real world, for negotiating their own wages, salaries, and/or raises. It teaches them to start valuing the contribution that they are making and gives them the confidence needed to believe that they are in control of their financial future. In this they have truly learned the art of being a financial superhero.

Conclusion

You've made it to the end of this book on how to train your kids to be Super Savers! Now is the time to go and use this information to start training your own financial superhero. This is an ongoing lesson, but if you didn't get the chance to start when your children were really young, don't worry... these lessons can be started at any age.

Make sure to focus more on what your child is learning, and at what pace, rather than focusing on the physical age of your child. We all learn at a different pace! Start slow, and keep it simple, working your way up to more complicated concepts as you go.

Super Savers

Becoming a Super Saver is more than just focusing on saving money. It is a lifetime learning of financial literacy and management that can start at a very young age, as long as you, as the parent, are dedicated to teaching your child what they need to succeed in life.

The steps set up within the *Super Savers* book are laid out in such a way to make the logical step from one concept to the next. As your child learns, and starts to become inquisitive about different financial aspects, you can certainly hop from one subject to another, as it fits where their interests lie, to keep it exciting for them. However, certain things may not make sense if you jump over some steps. You can explain to your child, "That is a good question… in order to understand it, let's take a look at this first…"

Everything you do should be geared toward keeping your child engaged and excited about earning and building for their future. Most of the activities in this book are laid out in such a way as to elicit that interest through the most visual and interactive ways possible. They are also easy to set up and implement, providing you the teaching tools to aid in your ability to engage your child.

Don't just sit down and lecture your child as a form of teaching them. Ask them questions and encourage them to ask any questions they may have. It is through your patience, and their understanding, that you are going to achieve the best results. If your child gets frustrated, stop to ask them questions about which part is causing their frustration, and don't just give them answers, help them work through to find the best solution that makes sense to them. Allow them to negotiate for changes to how you do things, as long as it gets them to the ultimate place you want them to be… a financial superhero capable of success throughout their lives.

The true point of working with your children is to help them become the responsible adults that you want

Super Savers

them to be. Through the lessons in this book, you will not only help deepen their understanding of how the world works from a financial perspective, but also deepen a long-lasting relationship of trust and respect between you and your child.

If you would like further information on teaching your child to become a financial superhero, check out the "Resources" section on our website at www.SuperSaversBook.com/resources. There you will find links to additional tools and information to help you teach your kids the concepts discussed in this book.

Remember that your kids aren't the only ones who can become financial Super Savers. You need to lead by example and be one yourself! You can also find more ways to reorganize and manage your own personal finances, plus additional tips and tricks to help your kids reach true financial independence at www.DailyDollarFinances.com.

www.ingramcontent.com/pod-product-compliance
Lightning Source LLC
Chambersburg PA
CBHW050006230526
45465CB00003BB/1280